HOW TO LEAD SOMEONE TO CHRIST

(How To Be Used Of God To See Someone Come To Faith In Christ)

James E. Watson, Ph.D.

Presbyterian Pastor

DEDICATION

Thanks to God for revealing Himself in creation (Rom.1:18-20) and in the hearts of people (Rom.2:14-15) and through His Son Jesus Christ and through His Word, which He has caused to be written by the Holy Spirit and preserved for us today. His same Spirit enables us to understand and live and share His Word in power.

Thanks to God for my family.

TABLE OF CONTENTS

CHAPTER 1

PRELIMINARY CONCERNS

Make sure you're a Christian

Before you seek to lead someone to Christ or to be used of God to see someone come to Christ, you need to make sure that you are a Christian. You need to make sure that you have repented and put your faith in Christ as Savior and Lord. You need to make sure that you understand that you are saved by grace and not by works. If you have any question about this, or even if you don't, it would probably be a good idea to turn to the chapter that deals with what it means to be a Christian in this book and look that over and make sure that you are a Christian.

Understand that God Saves People

Having established this, the first thing I want to say about leading a person to Christ is that we need to realize that people become Christians because God causes them to become a Christian. God is the one who convicts them of sin through the Holy Spirit. God is the one that enables them to have faith and to believe in Him. So it is a work of God to save a person and all we do is to be the instruments through whom God works to see people come to Christ. Let me share now some things that I've learned about how to lead people to Christ.

Try to Establish a Friendly Relationship with People
The first thing, if possible, is that you want to seek to establish a friendly relationship with people. What you can share with people when you don't know them versus what you can share with people when you do know them well is tremendously different. You can share how a person becomes a Christian with a person you don't even know and sometimes they will become Christians, but often the more you know a person the more they will listen to you and the more they will accept what you say. So I always try, if possible, to establish a friendly relationship with people and I try to figure out how long I'm going to have with these people. If I see someone and I just meet them on a plane or I see them somewhere and I expect I'll never see them again, I try to go ahead and witness to them as I have the opportunity and as they seem to be open in that situation. I'll try to lead the conversation around to becoming a Christian and share my testimony with them and I'll give them a tract – a brochure that explains how you become a Christian. But if I have a neighbor, for instance, that I hope over some time I may see again and again or have somebody that I expect to see because they cut my hair or work on my car, I may decide as I pray about it to just go slow and easy and let a relationship develop and then share Christ with them and tell them how to become a Christian as the opportunity develops. So first, I would seek to establish a relationship and this is really a hard thing to me. I tend to be aggressive. I tend to want to share Christ the minute I see somebody and so I have to pray that God would teach me how to be wise and learn to wait and know when to share the gospel. Should I speak now or should I let it go? I think of a person that I'm trying to witness to now, that I see sporadically. I try to go as far as I can with them in sharing Christ without them backing away. That's something you just learn or God just teaches you. Of course, people are different, so some you can seem to go a little further with and with others you sense a resistance, so you don't go very far. If you have relatives or people you already know, then you

can usually share the gospel with them much easier because you already have the relationship with them. So first, you try to establish a relationship from which to share the truth.

Be on the Lookout for People upon Whom God is Working
Another thing you would want to think about in sharing the gospel is to be sensitive to people who are interested in spiritual matters. You will come around some people and you will sense that they are interested in talking about becoming a Christian. They may ask you questions about it. And these people may be ready to go, they may be like the Ethiopian eunuch, ready to put their faith in Christ. If you are sensitive to them (these kinds of people), you can go ahead and share the gospel with them and see if they are ready to receive it. It is just a question of knowing what to say to them. So always have your antenna out, being sensitive, and asking the Holy Spirit to guide you. Sharing Christ with people is basically you being a Christian, going around walking in the Holy Spirit and then as you come across people, you're thinking, "Hmmm, I wonder if this person is a Christian"? You'll want to ask the questions or bring up the matters that will help you to get some sense of whether they're Christians or not.

What is it I'm Trying to Get Across?
Now you have a chance to share with them how a person can become a Christian. What are you going to do when you share? You may have someone say to you, "How do I become a Christian?" Or maybe you have worked up in your relationship to this place. Or maybe you meet someone for the first and maybe the last time. What would you say? First of all, in sharing with them how to become a Christian, you want to get the basics across, especially if you're not sure how much time you have, and how long you're going to be able to talk to this person. And what are the basics? Repentance and faith by grace. You want to tell them that a person

has to repent and put their faith in Jesus Christ as Savior and Lord and understand and believe it's by grace that you're saved and not by works. You want to share that with them. The gospel is that Jesus died on the cross for our sins and was raised the third day and was seen by many witnesses (I Cor.15: 3-8). We need to share the gospel (Christ died for our sins and was raised the third day) and how to appropriate what Christ did on the cross. Repentance and faith in Christ is how you appropriate what Christ did on the cross for your benefit. Paul told the Philippian jailer who asked what he might do to be saved to believe in the Lord Jesus Christ (Acts 16:31). Now you can talk with them after you establish that, about other things and go into those areas in more depth, but that's what you want to get across. I like to utilize my testimony, because my testimony is about how I didn't understand that you're saved by grace and not by works. I grew up in a church thinking that is what they were teaching, which they were not; but I thought that they were saying that if I was a good person, if I went to church, if I read the Bible, if I did the things a Christian is supposed to do, then that's how I could become a Christian. So that's what I did. I tried to be a Christian. I tried to live for Christ – hoping that would help me to become a Christian. I finally realized that I was not ever going to make it that way and I quit trying. I later heard in a sermon that you become a Christian by grace and not by works (Ephesians 2:8-9). All I had to do was to put my faith in Christ. Utilizing your testimony is a good way to bring the conversation around to what you want to share with the person.

Learn What to Say and How to Say it
The problem I see is that Christians don't understand what to share with a person about how to become a Christian. Once they learn what to say they have a hard time actually saying it. When you witness, you have to know what to say and then you have to be able to say it to them so that they can understand what you are saying.

You have to be able to explain it and make it clear to them and perhaps to illustrate it. Now if you don't know anything about what happened to you except that you believe in Jesus, then tell them that. The man in the gospel of John said, "all I know is once I was blind and now I can see." But you are a pretty blunt instrument in God's hands if that is all you can do. You want to be a sophisticated scalpel, not a rough spoon, for the surgery. You want to be a sophisticated scalpel that God can use in His hands to help a person to come to Christ. You should seek to be able to share with someone how they can become a Christian and allow them to interrupt you with questions as you proceed.

CHAPTER 2

HERE IS WHAT YOU ARE TRYING TO SHARE

If I am able, I explain the gospel by drawing it out. I have found that sharing the gospel verbally is subject to being misunderstood. They may not understand the words I am using. So I have found that if I can draw it out, it makes it clearer to people, and they seem to get the point of the gospel, especially grace. The first thing I do is to put God at the top of the page, then down at the left corner I put Adam and Eve. Then I draw a timeline across the page.

God

Adam & Eve
____

Then I say when God created Adam and Eve, everything was perfect. They were in a right relationship. Then Adam and Eve fell from the relationship with God when they sinned. Then I draw a little line dropping down below the timeline and all the way across, and point out that everybody, according to the Bible, has been born down on this level (except for Jesus).

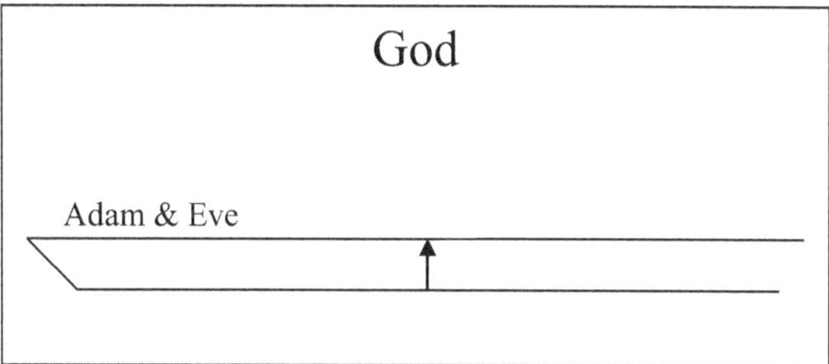

They have been born in sin separated from God. So when you seek to want to know God, you have to understand that you are not born in a right relationship with God but separated from God. So how then does a person get to know God? The first thing you have to do is to repent of your sin. You have to repent of being a sinner. What does it mean to repent? First, it means that you admit that you are a sinner. Secondly, it means having genuine sorrow over the realization that you are a sinner. Thirdly, it means to purpose to turn from sin, from your life of sin. Fourthly, repentance entails asking forgiveness for your sins.

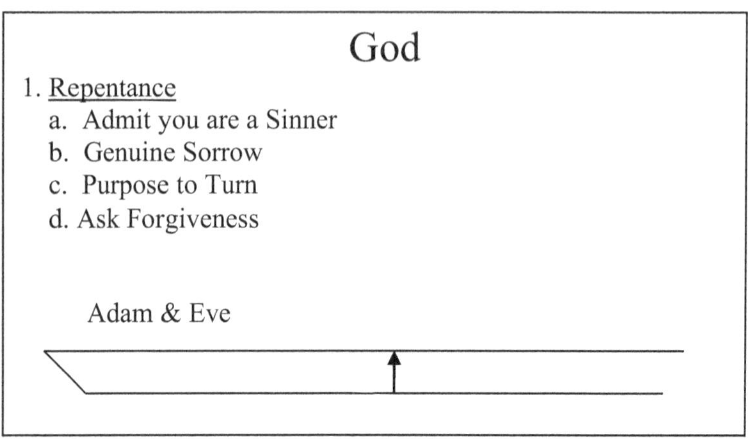

Repentance means admitting that you are a sinner. Everybody in the world is a sinner (except for Jesus), and we all have to admit that we are sinners. A sinner is not necessarily on the ten most wanted list, but a sinner is someone who is running their own life, rebelling against God. Someone said you could spell sin with a little "s" and a big "I" and a small "n". Sin means I want to run my own life. Because we want to run our own life, we are in rebellion against God and do things that are displeasing to Him, and these things are sins. Everybody is a sinner. Even good people are sinners. Some people say that they are not sinners, but that they are good persons. And they may be good, compared to other people. If you make a 60 on the test and everybody else makes a 40, you are better than they are, but you didn't make a 100. So under God's standard of what is right and wrong, we are all sinners. The Bible says all of us sin and fall short of the glory of God (Rom.3:23). Repentance is a u-turn. This is the big repentance from non-Christian to Christian. (Now as a Christian you repent of individual sins, i.e., you admit that this sin is wrong, and that you are sorry about it and that you are purposing not to do it again and you ask God to forgive this sin. I call this repentance of individual sins as a Christian little repentance, to differentiate it from the big repentance from non-Christian to Christian). Next they have to understand that they are saved by grace and not by works. I draw a little passage-way from God to man and note that God is up here and we are down there at the bottom of the passage-way.

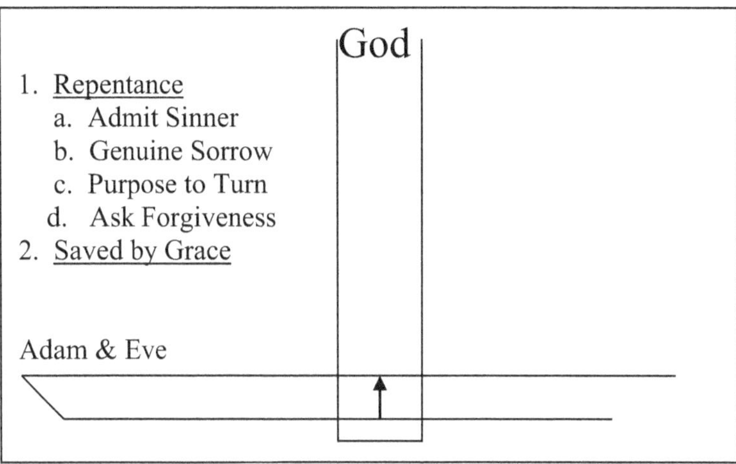

If we stay there we end up in hell forever. But we can't get ourselves out, so what are we going to do? Well, we can't do anything. God reaches down and draws us up.

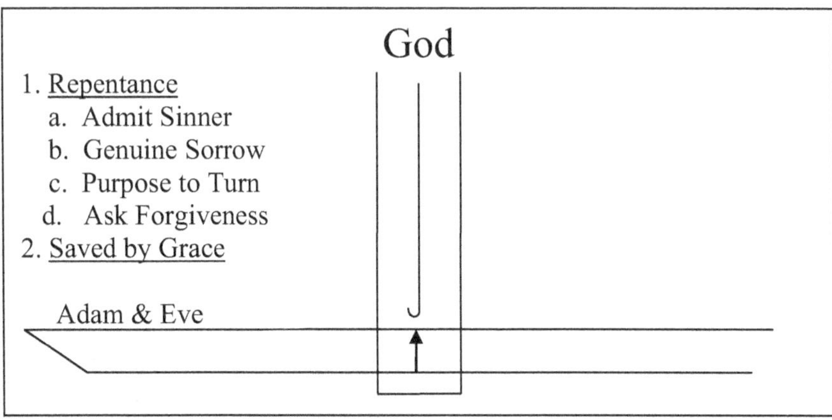

Then I draw the cross across that passageway showing that is how God loves us and sends His son to die for us. It is by grace we are saved. Grace means unmerited favor, (and there I will share my testimony about how I didn't know that we are saved by grace, thinking that we are saved by works). God sent Jesus to die for us. So it is a top down operation; it is not from the bottom up. The third thing I explain is that Jesus is the only way to be saved. I also emphasize here that Jesus is God, the Son of God. He is God and man as the Bible portrays Him.

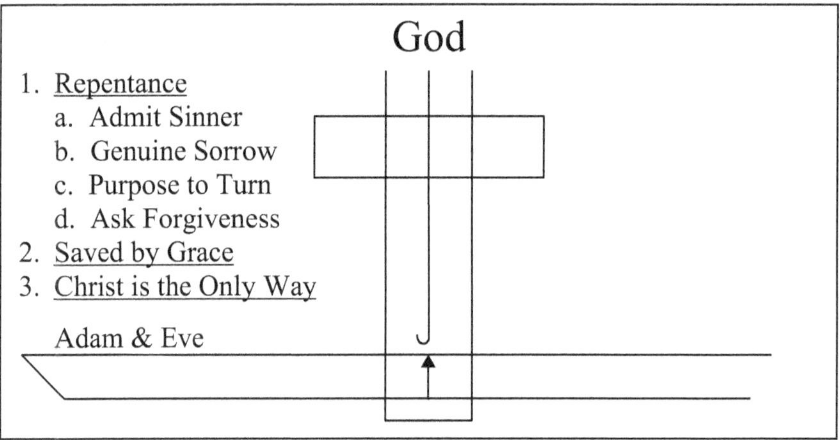

They have to understand and believe that Jesus is God, God's Son, and He is the only way to be saved. I explain that this is the only way because it is the way of justice, where God has provided a way. He has provided a sacrifice for our sins to satisfy His justice and His wrath. And this is the only way that justice is satisfied. That is why it is the only way. Jesus said, "I am the way, the truth, and the life. No man comes to the Father but through me." (John 14:6) It is open to all people to come. It is open to all, so people can't say they couldn't get in that way. Fourthly, (I write all this in the left-hand column at the top of the page)

to become a Christian you have to accept Christ as Savior and Lord by faith.

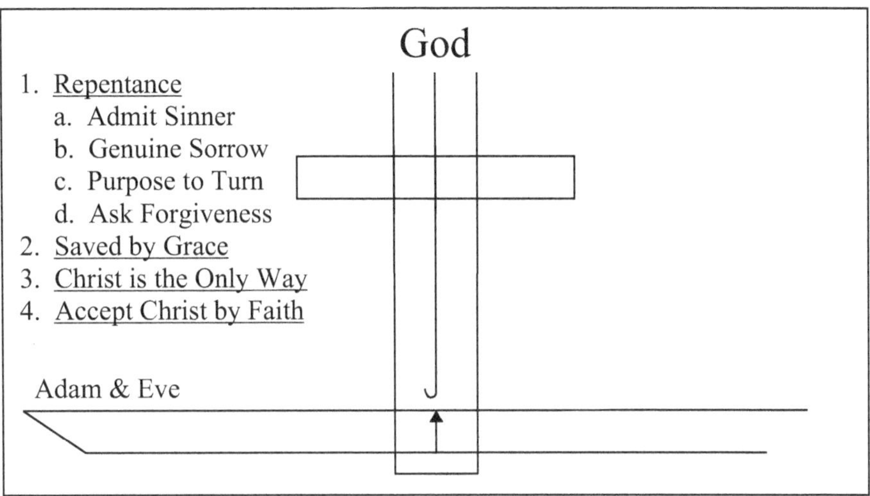

What do we have to do to become Christians?

We have to repent and have faith. Faith in Christ as Savior and Lord. What does that mean to have faith? It means a little bit of knowledge – that you understand it is by grace and not by works. It means to trust Christ, to trust that His death will get you to Heaven. Faith means knowledge, trust, and belief. You believe in Jesus as the Son of God Who died for our sins. It means that you are committing your life to Jesus Christ as Savior and Lord of your life, seeking to make Him the boss of your life. It is a faith that commits itself, it is a committing kind of faith.

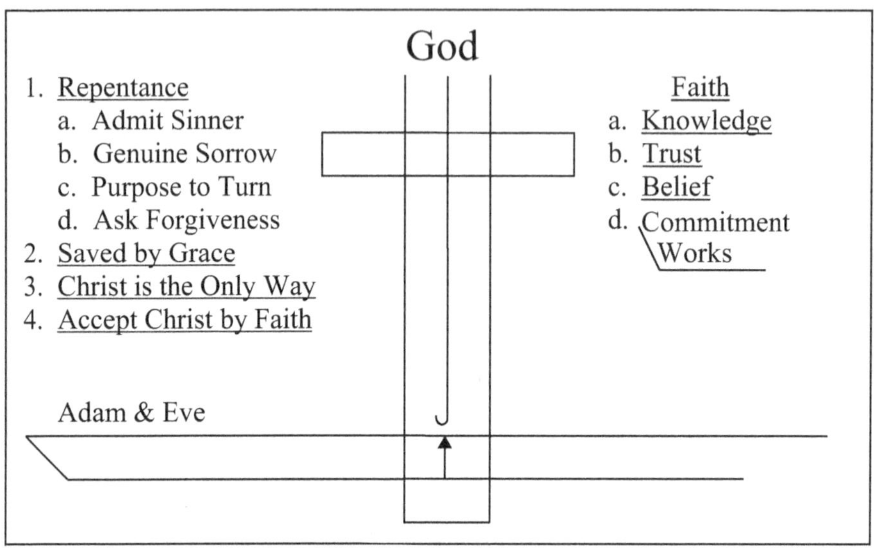

Where do works come in? Your works are the evidence of this faith and this commitment. If you don't have works, then that is a sign that you are not a Christian. James said faith without works is dead. So you have to have works, to give evidence of your faith. Works don't save you. They don't keep you saved. But they are the evidence of your being saved. If you adopted a child, you wouldn't say "I will adopt you if you will make up your bed." But you would say that you want them to make up their bed. Why? Because they are your child. They make up their bed not in order to become your child or to stay your child, but because they are your child. You don't do good works to become a child of God or to stay a child of God, but because you are a child of God. Commitment to Christ means that you are seeking to do His will. It doesn't mean that you will do His will perfectly, but that you will have this kind of commitment to Him as the boss of your life. The Bible teaches that you must take Christ as Lord of your life to become a Christian. In Matthew 7:22-23, Jesus said, "Many will say…Lord, Lord…and I will declare to them, I never knew you; depart from me you who practice lawlessness."

What do you do after you Share it?

As you present this, it is good to let them ask you questions. If not, just do it the best way you can. Don't get sidetracked. They may want to know about predestination. I just tell them enough to satisfy them until I can get through the gospel. If they are not Christians, they will never understand predestination. Even Christians may not understand predestination. So what you want to do is to help them to come to Christ and then things like this the Lord can help them to have a peace about and understand as much as they can or will. But if a person is sincerely interested in an answer, I'll try to give them an answer that satisfies them.

First ask if they understood it

After you have finished going through the presentation, ask if they understood it. If yes, then I proceed. If not, ask what they didn't understand, and then go over again what they didn't understand

Go over it again – making sure they understand

I go over these things again to see if they understood repentance, grace, Jesus being the only way, and Jesus being God. I believe we should be very thorough here. Often people will have questions or a lack of understanding. Then I go over faith and what faith means; i.e., trust, belief, commitment. I am not trying to see if they believe it, I am just trying to see if they understand it.

Next see if they have done it

Now I go over each point to see if they not only understand the point, but whether they have actually done each aspect of becoming a Christian. Have they repented? Do you believe it is by grace? Do you believe that Jesus is God's Son, the only way to know Him? Do you believe in Jesus and have you put your faith in Him? Have you made this kind of commitment? In this way you can figure out where they are. I do this in a nice way, letting them use this presentation as a self-diagnostic tool.

What if they have done it?
It may be that they say, I have done all this. Good, then we can assume they are Christians.

What if they are ready to become a Christian?
If they are ready to become a Christian, we will move ahead and let them pray and ask Christ into their life.

What if they have some problems?
But if they have some problem areas such as being unwilling to repent, or not believing that Jesus is the only way and that He is God's Son, or being unwilling to make a commitment to Christ, then they are not ready to pray to receive Christ as Savior and Lord. I may go over it again if I am not sure they understand it clearly. I don't want them to reject something they may misunderstand. If they have not done it, I might ask what is keeping them from doing it, and sometimes it takes an explanation to help them. If they have problems with Jesus being the only way and are concerned about non-Christians being lost, I point out that Jesus said He is the only way in the Bible. They will have to decide if they believe the Bible. If they are not willing to make a commitment, some people may say, "I'm kind of afraid to, I don't know what God might do with me." Of course the old answer for that is that if you give yourself to God, He is going to do the best thing for you. If your children said, "I'll do what you want me to do, Dad or Mother," wouldn't you do the best for them? God will bless those who commit their lives to Him. It is the best thing in the world to have somebody so wise and knowledgeable running your life. People sometimes have to be encouraged in these different areas. So I go over it with them and make sure they understand it clearly and correctly.

What if they are not ready?

They may not be ready to pray to receive Christ. I try to keep the relationship going, if possible. I continue to pray for them. I encourage them to come to church, and I encourage them to study the Bible. God is going to bring them to the point of salvation (if they are saved), not me. All I want to do is see where they are and where they need to get to. I want them to come to church and listen to the Bible, and let the Holy Spirit work on them. Faith comes by hearing and hearing through the Word of Christ (Romans 10:17). We had one Jewish man come to church for five years before he was converted. Now he is keeping on with Christ, and is a teacher and elder in the church. With some people it takes time. We just seek to love people as God brings them into His Kingdom. It is important, I might add here, for you to have a church. It is important for a church to be a place where non-Christians can come and hear the gospel and hear it as long as they need to hear it until they become Christians. Without affirming them and saying they have right lifestyles and beliefs, we can let them know we love them and accept them where they are, so God can work on them through this loving environment. You want to have a church situation where it is seeker-sensitive. You are sensitive to these people. You are kind to them. You are careful what you say in front of them in terms of speaking derogatorily about people who are not Christians. In preaching I share God's truth, and try to speak the truth in love. But I am aware that there are non-Christians sitting there listening who don't have the Holy Spirit in them and don't understand everything. So we just try to let them know we love them and we understand where they are and want them to come to Christ.

What if they are ready to become a Christian?

But what if they haven't done it, and they are just now understanding it and they are willing to do this? I don't try to talk them out of it, but I do try to make sure they are really serious about this commitment.

I seek to impress upon them the seriousness of this commitment to Christ. I explain that they should be sincere. They should understand what it means to become a Christian. That is why we just went over this. They have to believe this is true. If you don't believe it, then how can you make a commitment to it. Then I say to them, "Would you like to pray to receive Christ now or later?" A good way to express their relationship with Christ is to pray and ask Christ into their life. This way they can remember when they prayed to receive Christ. Also, it helps them to have somebody like me around them when they pray to receive Christ. I can affirm to them when the devil wants them to think that they are not Christians, that they prayed with me to receive Christ. If they are ready, I try to encourage them to pray to receive Christ. I don't want them to feel coerced. I want the Holy Spirit to be working on them so that they want to do this.

If they are ready lead them in prayer (if they wish)
If they are ready to pray and ask Christ into their life, I ask if they want me to lead them in prayer or would they rather go home and do it. Usually people will tell me they would rather pray with me, because they want to make sure they do it right. I ask if they want to pray out loud or silently. Most people will pray out loud and basically all you do is just pray a simple prayer. I tell them in advance what we are going to do. I will pray a prayer and they just repeat after me. I will say a little phrase and then they repeat that phrase. I just pray a prayer that is similar to this:

How to Pray

> "Lord, I admit that I am a sinner. I repent of my sins, and put my faith in Christ as Savior and Lord. I believe that Jesus is the Son of God and Savior of sinners. I believe Jesus died upon the cross for my sins. I believe that you are saved by grace and not by works. In Jesus name, Amen.

AFTERWARD

Then I encourage them that they have done the right thing. I remind them that they need to grow as a Christian. They should try to have a time of Bible reading and prayer each day. They should seek to study the Bible. They should become integral in a Bible-teaching church. In one week I meet with them again to follow them up. If you lead someone to Christ you are responsible for their follow-up, so don't just let them pray to receive Christ with you and go off and not have any follow-up. They need that support. Just like when you buy a computer and you have support to tell you how to work it and how to deal with problems, they need that support spiritually. So when I meet with them one week later, I go over how to become a Christian again. I do basically the same thing we did when they prayed to receive Christ (without the prayer to receive Christ), and just remind them of what they have done. It helps them clear up questions. Then in the next few weeks, I make sure they know certain basics of Christian growth. I might share a little guideline for prayer, like ACTS – adoration, confession, thanksgiving, supplication. I will share with them how to repent of sins, how to have daily devotions, how to walk in the Holy Spirit, and how to have assurance of salvation. How do they know they are Christians? One way is logically, that is they have done what the Bible says about how you become a Christian. Another way to know they are saved is experientially. As they grow they should see a change in their life such as I John speaks of, i.e. love for fellow Christians, confessing Christ as the Son of God, acting like a Christian, and having the Holy Spirit in them. If not by you, make sure that they are discipled by someone else. Someone who can keep up with them until they get to be mature Christians. Make sure they get involved in a good church. If they have never been baptized, they should be baptized. If they have never made a public profession of faith in Christ, they should do so. In our church you do that when you are baptized. Then I make sure they are in church. I tell them that there are some things you do, not in order to become a Christian, but because you are a Christian. These are baptism, a public confession of Christ, good works, and church membership. God has called us as Christians to share our faith. Jesus said to go and make disciples. I encourage you as a Christian to trust God and help people become Christians, as the Holy Spirit guides you. It is a blessing to be used of God.

I have found giving people you are witnessing to a tract with your contact information on it a valuable tool in witnessing. Below is the tract I use, feel free to copy and use it (with your contact information, or mine if you want them to talk with me)

Becoming a Christian requires 4 things according to the Bible: 1) Repentance – admitting you are a sinner (someone who is trying to run your own life), and purposing – by God's grace – to live as God would have you live. 2) Grace – salvation is a gift from God in that God sent Jesus to die on the cross for our sins and pay the price we couldn't pay. So we don't earn or deserve our salvation, but must believe it is achieved by Christ's death on the cross for us. 3) Jesus - believing that Jesus is the only way to be saved, and that He is both God and man. 4) Faith – involves belief, trust, and commitment to Christ as Savior and Lord. Our good works, i.e., going to church, trying to live a holy life, etc., are the results of being a Christian, they don't make us a Christian. Commitment to Christ as Lord doesn't mean we will lead a perfect life, but that we will strive to live for Him and repent when we fail.

If you have been enabled to believe in Jesus by the power of the Holy Spirit and would like to commit your life to Him as Savior and Lord, you can sincerely and seriously pray this prayer as a way of making that commitment to Christ: "Lord, I admit that I am a sinner. I repent of my sins. I want to put my faith in Jesus as Savior and Lord. I believe that Jesus is God and man, and that He died on the cross for my sins and was raised the third day. I believe that salvation is by grace and not by works." If you prayed that prayer, or need help in becoming or growing as a Christian, you can contact me, Jim Watson, at jimwatson44@yahoo.com.

ABOUT THE AUTHOR

James E. Watson is a retired Presbyterian pastor, with a B.A. in biology from King University, an M.Div. from Columbia Theological Seminary, and a Ph.D. from Florida State University in Humanities. Contact him at jimwatson44@yahoo.com